How To Change
The World Without Breaking
A Sweat

A Practical Guide to Leading
and Managing People

Joel W. Bunkowske, Esq.
J.D., M.B.A.

First Edition

Published by Idealist Media

Copyright © 2015 Joel W. Bunkowske

All rights reserved.

ISBN: 147817112X

ISBN-13: 978-1478171126

"THERE IS NOTHING NEW UNDER THE SUN"

Ecclesiastes 1:9

This book is built on the shoulders of giants and incorporates the ideas and concepts of the authoritative leadership and psychology researchers, practitioners, and trainers including; Plato, Aristotle, Carl Jung, Isabel Briggs Myers and Katharine Cook Briggs, Lawrence Kohlberg, Albert Ellis, Stephen Covey, Jim Collins, Marcus Buckingham and Curt Coffman, Brian Tracy, Tony Alessandra, and the most profound leadership trainer of all time, Jesus Christ. My contribution was choosing what ideas to include and how the ideas are presented.

DEDICATION

This book is dedicated to my wonderful wife Susan Bunkowske. Thank you for all of our deep discussions on human behavior. You are truly a partner in my thinking, teaching, and writing.

Thanks to all of my students all over the United States. You have allowed me to hone my thinking on leading and managing people. Thanks to Susan Bunkowske, Eugene Bunkowske, and Crystal Turner for proofreading the manuscript.

CONTENTS

INTRODUCTION

As I think about the great successes of the Western World and the challenges that face humanity, I realize that the only lasting competitive advantage comes from maximizing human potential. Human potential is that last great opportunity for the creation of wealth. It is a giant trove of treasure just waiting to be uncovered. The magical elixir will propel the world from scarcity thinking into the enlightened and innovative new world of global cooperation.

In his book The Wealth of Nations, Adam Smith shared the insight that when nations specialize and trade they all become richer. Mass communications allows us to share knowledge globally at the click of a button. As we move from a competitive paradigm to a cooperative worldview we can raise the standard of living for all human beings and the noble goals of the eradication of hunger, poverty and financial servitude can finally be achieved.

1

MAXIMIZING HUMAN POTENTIAL

For much too long the world has embraced the wrong kind of leader. Our model has been one of the great, visionary, all-knowing genius who has a magical gift for leadership. This concept has led us to search for that special gifted individual who will take us from mediocrity to greatness. We search high and low for these special people. We differentiate through grading systems in school. We apply a bell curve that stratifies human beings for the purpose of uncovering the great among us. We offer massive salaries, rewards and special privileges to entice the people we believe are worthy into positions of leadership. However, all too often, we realize that success is created by external forces and not by the genius of leaders.

I believe that stratification, incentives, and special privileges have not brought us the sustainable rewards that we expected. I believe that we have wasted valuable resources and energy pursuing a wrong-minded ideology. The truth is that all human beings have the ability to lead. As we learn to maximize human potential, we will see an exponential growth explosion in wealth unlike anything the world has ever seen.

As I present seminars all across the United States, I ask participants if they are being fully utilized at work. I ask them whether they believe that they could be more productive if they were given greater responsibility, authority, and resources. The answer is always a resounding "YES!" From janitor to manager, the vast majority of people believe that they could be better utilized by their employer and more productive in the workplace.

The reason we are not maximizing human potential is that we believe that human beings are the tools to bring about the vision of genius leaders. When we talk to these leaders, if they are honest, they admit that they do not have any special insights or mysterious understanding beyond what is available to all people through education and experience. What leaders do is gamble on their ideas. Sometimes they are successful and sometimes they are not. If they are lucky, they have more successes than failures and they are widely admired as geniuses.

The more we look at the concept of leadership, the more we realize that the truly successful leaders are the ones who build cooperative teams. They empower the team with authority to act and rely on the team to create success. This is the only way to create a sustainable success beyond the tenure of the leader.

Truly great organizations create systems that build and maximize the potential of future leaders. In this way, they systematically create a sustainable rejuvenation of leadership. I suggest that this philosophy needs to be applied to the entire organization to obtain the explosion in wealth creation that I am talking about.

The concept of management needs to be completely turned around. The most important people in any organization are frontline workers. The job of top management is not to be visionary geniuses but instead to discover, organize, teach, train, mentor, build, and maximize the potential of all human beings in the organization.

The idea that it is enough for an organization to carry out the will and vision of the CEO is no longer good enough. Management has a responsibility to maximize the potential of the organization beyond the limitations of one human mind. Management must unleash the incredible innovative potential of all the individuals in an organization from janitor to chairman of the board of directors.

Naturally, I am expecting a great deal more out of managers with this philosophy. I know that managers are much more capable then they have ever been allowed to be in traditional hierarchical organizations. The potential of managers has not been maximized. Most managers have been taught that using their own minds and ideas leads to negative consequences in organizations where the purpose of the organization is to fulfill the vision of the "genius" leader.

Understanding how to maximize human potential requires that we understand how the human mind works. We must know why people do the things that they do. We must know why some people are not eager to participate. We must know why some people are lazy. We must know why some people bring negative attitudes to work. We must know why some people do not believe they can be successful. We must know why some people feel that they do not deserve success.

2

COMPETENCE, COMMUNITY AND PRODUCTIVITY

I always say that the art of management is nothing but the art of relationship. Most people do not understand this and spend much of their time in a futile attempt to force people to do the things they would like them to do through the hierarchical management approach.

The hierarchical management approach is one where and manager says to the employee, "Do your job or I will fire you." When we use the hierarchical management approach, we are using the emotion of fear to get the job done. "Be very afraid, I have all the power you do not. You are a completely replaceable piece of machinery. You are of no importance to the organization. I will replace you anytime I believe you are not doing what I expect of you."

When leaders use this form of management, it creates an "us-versus-them" atmosphere. In an "us-versus-them" atmosphere, employees resent management. This causes them to do the least amount work they can get by with while complaining all the time that they are not being paid enough money. Employees are not committed to the organization or to the manager, and they are not highly productive.

Naturally, this situation is one that is unsound in the long run. What we need is a form of management where the employees are connected to the organization, and they realize that they are extremely important. The employees have jobs that they are competent to do and that they enjoy. They realize that their work is vital to the success of the organization. Using this style of management creates what we call a new management environment. It is based on the concept of total quality management.[1]

In a total quality environment, we seek to have statistically zero defects in manufacturing and zero complaints about our service. When using the hierarchical management approach, where fear is the main motivator, when the manager is not there to oversee the employees, some employees will work at a much less productive rate than when the manager is there to oversee the work. We all know the old saying, "When the cat is away, the mice will play." Often, this is because the employee resents the power that management holds over them. Where there is resentment, a productive work environment will never be achieved.

The only way to create a highly productive work force is through the empowerment of the employee. The empowered employee is one that feels totally connected to the organization. The employee realizes that the manager cares for the employee as a human being and the organization is organized to nurture human

---

[1] Deming (2000)

potential. The way we do this is through delegation, teaching, training, and mentoring.

When we delegate work to an employee that is just a little more difficult than the work they are doing currently, the employee will have to learn a new skill to achieve success. When we teach the employee a new skill, they gain competence. This increased sense of competence increases the employee's sense of self-esteem. As the self-esteem of the employee is increased, the productivity of the employee will also increase because we find that high self-esteem in employees correlates to high productivity.

We understand that to increase the sense of competence in an employee, we use delegation, but there is another important element to increase self-esteem and create a highly productive work force. That is the sense of community.

When we speak about the sense of community at work, what we mean is that an employee feels accepted and at home in the work environment. They enjoy feelings of belonging. They sense that people care about them as human beings. When they work hard, their manager praises them and shows respect for their commitment. When they have too much work to do, other employees will pitch in and help them instead of saying "That's not in my job description." When others have too much work, they will return the favor and help the busy person out.

The opposite of having a good sense of community would be where employees come to work and feel uncomfortable. They work hard for the organization but there is no praise from their manager. People gossip about each other. They stab each other in the back verbally and do not help one another.

3

CHOOSING THE RIGHT TEAM

In his book Good to Great[2], Jim Collins says that we need to get the right people on the bus in the right seat and get the wrong people off the bus. Naturally, the bus is our organization, and the seats on the bus are the positions in the organization. Jim Collins does not spend much time on how to get the right person in the right seat on the bus; therefore, I would like to help us understand this very important function of management.

The single most important thing one can do to maximize success in an organization is to choose the right team. Most people choose their team using a

---

[2] Collins (2001)

shotgun method. The candidate arrives for an interview, shows a lot of enthusiasm, and we hire them based on their resume. We put the employee in the job without any real understanding of their natural gifts and talents. It is quite possible that the employee will succeed, but it is just as common to find that the employee took the job merely for the money and there never was a good fit.

I believe that it is much better to hire people based on temperament. Temperament is a field of study that started with the ancient Greeks, Plato, and Aristotle. It was further expanded upon by Carl Jung and again expanded upon by Myers-Briggs, a mother-daughter team that created a temperament test called the Myers-Briggs Type Indicator®.[3]

The Myers-Briggs Type Indicator is a brilliant test that tells us why we are the way we are. It is widely used and if you take the test, you will be amazed. When you get your results, you will say to yourself, "That is exactly the way I am. How on earth did they know?" The

---

[3] Myers (1998)

Myers-Briggs Type Indicator identifies 16 categories of temperament. The only problem with the Myers-Briggs Type Indicator is that tells you a lot about yourself but it does not tell you about anyone else.

The only way you can get to know about your employee is if they take the test, tell you their temperament, and you read about their temperament which is time consuming in the workplace. Other researchers have put together different temperament tests that modify the original Myers-Briggs categories. Although the Myers-Briggs Type Indicator is probably the most powerful temperament test, currently available, other systems of classification can be used as easier ways to hire the right people and put them in the right job.

The form of temperament test I describe here and suggest you use in your hiring practices has four basic categories. Different practitioners have explained these categories using different names for the four categories. Dr. Tony Alessandra developed the system I use. The four categories of temperament we will use are directors, socializers, relaters, and thinkers.[4]

We have to realize that because we are you using only four categories of temperament, some people can bridge between two temperaments. Also, as we spend more time on the planet, many of us realize that the other temperaments have ways of looking at the world that are good to adopt as we begin to learn to see the world from other people's perspectives. Let us discuss each of the four types.

DIRECTORS

Directors are direct, self-contained and assessing. They are bottom-line people. They need to succeed since their self-image is often based on how successful they are. They are scheduled people. They know when they will wake up the morning, when they will get to the office, when their first meeting is, when their second meeting is, etc. They have their entire day scheduled out, their entire week scheduled out, their entire month scheduled out, their entire year scheduled out. If they are strong directors, they may even be scheduled for up to three years in advance.

---

[4] Alessandra (1996)

They are the kind of people who enjoy work and are very good at it. If they are being paid to work for eight hours, they will put in nine hours and not ask to be paid for the extra hour. They take work home and are very comfortable working on weekends. When they get into upper management, they will take a cell phone on vacation and call the office three times a day because they cannot stand to be away from the action. Because they are such hard workers, they often rise very quickly to positions of responsibility in organizations.

If you have a director for a boss, do not go to meeting with them half an hour early. If you do, you will be butting into their last meeting. Be ready to leave the meeting exactly when it is scheduled to be over. If you ask for a half hour to be tacked on the end of the meeting, what you are really doing is throwing off their schedule for the next three years.

When you go into a meeting with a director do not waste time. They are very busy people who want to get right to the bottom line.

One of the best things you can do for a director is to come into the meeting prepared. Write a one-page memo to present at the meeting. At the top of the memo write out what problem needs to be solved at the meeting. Write out three possible solutions A, B, and C. Write out the pros and cons of each solution. At the bottom of the page write out the solution that you think is best and explain why it is best. A director will appreciate your effort. They will read your memo and quickly make a decision on which way to proceed after asking you a short series of questions.

If you get into the details to deeply, the director will say, "Hold on, I'm not interested in all the details. That is what I hired you to figure out. Here is the strategy and the goal. You can figure out how to do this in any way you feel comfortable as long as you achieve the results I have set out." This tendency of directors not to micromanage makes them extremely good leaders. Of all the temperaments, the extroverted director often makes a natural born leader.

Within each of the temperaments, we find unique strengths and weakness. The weakness of the director is that in their march to get to the bottom-line they often march right over their people. They are "bottom line oriented" people not "people oriented people." The good news is that directors who understand new management theory can overcome this weakness. Once they realize that the way to create productive employees is to increase their sense of competence and community, they quickly embrace new management theory. If you have a director for a boss who understands new management theory, not only does your business runs smooth as silk, but it becomes a wonderful and challenging place to work where people are treated fairly and well rewarded for success.

SOCIALIZERS

Socializers are direct, open, and accepting. They are the kind of people that come to a party and within ten minutes, they are the life of the party. They love to talk and they are very good at it. Very strong socializers talk so much we can hardly get a word in edgewise. Socializers are generally touchy-feely. When they talk to you, they pat your hand, your arm, or your shoulder. They will give you a hug at the drop of the hat.

Socializers are the kind of people that you drop off in a foreign land and within twenty minutes, they have twenty new friends even though they do not speak the local language. Socializers have the highest level of what we call emotional intelligence. Emotional intelligence is the ability to connect with other people.

Say I want to buy a car. I go onto a car lot and the salesperson who greets me is as socializer. I say to the socializer, "I see you have a ten thousand dollar almost new truck that is perfect for my budget." The socializer will say, "Let's go look at it." Halfway down the car lot, I walk by a thirty thousand dollar brand new sports car. The socializer says, "Do you want to sit in the sports car?" I say, "No, it's out of my price range." The socializers says, "Don't worry about it; I know you won't buy it. You can just sit in it for fun." I say, "As long as you know I won't buy it, I'll check it out for fun."

I sit in the sports car and immediately the socializer sniffs the air. I sniff the air and smell that wonderful new-car smell. The socializer says, "How do you feel in that leather seat? It's heated you know." They turn on the seat warmer. I say, "Wow, that's wonderful, just like a massage." The socializer says, "Check out the surround sound stereo system." They turn on the stereo. I say, "It's just like a concert hall in here." The socializer says, "Look at all those people, they're checking you out in this fancy car." By now, I am excited about the sports car. Thirty minutes later, I am driving out in a brand-new car I just bought from my brand-new friend on credit, and I am happy about it. It is amazing; socializers can get you to do just about anything they want. They have this natural ability to connect to our emotions and get us to do the things down deep we really want to do. This makes socializers the best salespeople for non-technical sales.

I ask the socializers to balance my checkbook. Within one hundred dollars either way is balanced to most socializers if it gets balance at all! This is because they do not care very much for details. How do details help them with interpersonal relationships? They do not. Therefore, I hire a socializer. I put them in an eight foot by ten-foot room with no windows, no people, no phones, and ask them do data entry all day. What happens? They bounce around that room, they cannot stand being alone, and soon they quit, or they flit around from office to office all day socializing. The last three hours of the day, they try to get eight hours of work done and make all kinds of mistakes.

As their manager, I look at the work they have done the next morning and notice the mistakes. I ask them why there are so many mistakes. They immediately say, "I got the work done." They are not that concerned that the numbers actually mean something and must be right. Detail challenged is what I call them. It is not that they cannot deal with details they just do not like details and they rush through their work so they can get back to socializing.

RELATERS

Relaters are indirect, open, and accepting. They are your tried-and-true employees. When you asked them to do something, you never have to asked them twice and get it done. You ask them to do some overtime work for you. No problem, they will do it. You ask them to work on the weekend for you. No problem, they will do it. You ask them to give up their vacation for you. No problem, they will do it. Why? Because they care so much about the relationship that they do not want to let you down. To let you down would hurt the relationship. That is the last thing they want to do.

Relaters are the nicest type of people. They care deeply about others. They build deep close relationships with other people at work. They dislike conflict and strive to create an environment that is supportive for all members of the group. If you are a manager who is a relater, your biggest challenge is doing discipline. You hate doing discipline because discipline hurts the relationship.

Relaters often get work reversed delegated to them by their employees. This happens when your employee who is "dumb as a fox" stops by your desk at 1 p.m. and says, "I'm going on vacation and my plane leaves at 3:00 p.m. today. The problem is I have fourteen reports that I cannot finish them today. Do you think you could do them for me?" You say, "No problem, have a great vacation." You are so nice but you end up working all evening doing their work. They have just reverse delegated to you. They have also learned that you are a wonderful manager who will do all the work that they do not want to do.

They come back from vacation and soon they start having all kinds of reasons why they cannot do their work. They have emergencies at home, they have to pick up their child early from day care, or they need a day off because they are too stressed out. They start dropping off work on your desk as they walk out the door just assuming that you will do it for them.

If this is happening to you, you need to nip it in the bud. When they say, "I'm going on vacation and I couldn't get to these fourteen reports. Will you do them for me?" What you need to say is, "Don't worry about it. Have a great vacation. Those reports can wait. They'll be on your desk when you get back." You need to delegate back to the reverse delegator. If the reports cannot wait, you may have to say, "I guess you did some bad planning. You had better call the airline and change your flight. You can't leave until after work hours because there's no one here to do the work for you." This will be very difficult for relaters to do. The solution to the problem is assertive behavior.

Assertive behavior is imperative to success in management. Assertiveness is the ability to get things done without making enemies. Assertive people stand up for their own rights while respecting the rights of others. Assertiveness training is necessary for all managers and it is especially important for relaters.

THINKERS

Thinkers are indirect, self-contained and assessing. If you have managed many people, at some point you have managed a thinker. The thinker is the person you over generalize to by saying, "You're always late to work." The thinker will say, "Oh no, you are wrong. Two weeks ago on Friday I was 4.5 minutes early, you've been inconsistent with your data, and you're lying." For thinkers, accuracy with data is very

JOEL W. BUNKOWSKE

important. When people over generalize, from the thinker's worldview, they are lying.

Thinkers are people who get most of their excitement in life from their thought process. They are generally quite introverted and often keep to themselves. Sometimes we come to work and ask a thinker how their weekend was. They look at us with a big scowl on their face. The reason they are scowling is not that they do not like us; they are just frustrated because we intruded into their thought process.

If you have any technology that you enjoy, thank a thinker. They invented most of it. Thinkers are great computer programmers, inventors, architects, and engineers. They are incredible at anything to do with details. When you ask a thinker to make a quick decision they will say, "Let's get more data and study the subject, I'll get you the perfect answer in two months." The one thing a thinker hates is the possibility of being wrong.

I take my thinker employee; put them in an eight foot by ten-foot room with no windows, no people, and no phones. I asked them to write my computer program for me. What happens? They say, "Finally some peace and quiet. I can do my work without anyone interrupting me." Moreover, your computer program is flawless.

I take my thinker and put them in a non-technical sales position where they have to schmooze people all day long. How does that go? It does not. So I say to my thinker employee, "You bad employee. You are the worst salesperson I have. You are going to have to go to a week of sales school." How does that work? It does not work very well. The thinker employee comes back from sales school and still hates to schmooze people. So instead, I decide to send my thinker employee to computer programming school. How does that go? It works very well because the work fits the employee's temperament.

4

THE RIGHT PERSON FOR THE JOB

Say I take my top superstar socializer salesperson who is not good with details and say to them, "You bad employee, your reports are always a mess. I am sending to you to a week of detail school." My socializer salesperson goes off to a week of detail school. When they get back are they good with details? No, they just made many friends.

What I decide to do instead is to send my socializer salesperson to week of sales school. How does that go? They come back an absolute sales superstar because not only do they have the temperament for the job, but now they have learned great sales techniques. The point here is that we need to train on strengths and minimize weaknesses.

Each of your employees is an absolute superstar at something. Even you are laziest employee has a natural gift. Now that gift might be playing basketball. However, if an individual is great at basketball, maybe they should go and work for a sports team, or at the gym or at a sporting goods store. Wouldn't they be good at the work that involves the things that they think and care about naturally?

I have found that most people do not understand what their gift is. When I ask people what their gift is, many people say things like typing. Is typing a gift or a skill? I suggest that it is a skill, something that you learn. A gift is something that is innate, you are born with it. Sure, you can develop your gift, but it will come naturally.

If you want to know what your gift is, just think about the things that are natural for you. It is the things that you think about and care about. The things that seem so simple for you, it feels like cheating. A friend of mine has a master's degree in social work. When she was in school, she would say to me, "Studying social work is so easy for me, it seems so intuitive." I told tell her the reason studying social work was so easy for her was because she has a natural talent for it. There were many people in her classes that struggled just to get by with Cs.

Many people also discount their natural gifts. They say, "This is too easy. I'll try something that is more challenging." And they pursue their weakness instead of their strengths. In the United States, we have an American value that most people accept. It is that anyone with enough training and effort can achieve anything. We often hear people say, "If at first you don't succeed try, and try again." When we understand temperament, it becomes clear that this is not always the truth. Since people have strengths and weaknesses, it is imperative that we help people find their strengths so they can use those strengths for their work instead of the weaknesses.

CHILDREN AND TEMPERAMENT

Say you have a child who is a strong socializer. They love to talk and are great with interpersonal communications but they hate details. They are kinesthetic, that is they love to do hands-on things like sports. This makes them struggle with math and science. Because we believe that anyone can achieve success with enough effort we often think that the child must not be trying. So we tell them to try harder. "If you would just try harder, you would be good at math and science." We verbally bully the child thinking that they are just being lazy and not obeying. The problem here is not laziness. It is a temperament problem.

The child is just not naturally wired to care about details. All the way through high school, the child endures verbal assaults on their self-esteem. After they graduate from high school, they get a job. If they get the right job, they will find that their communication skills are very valuable. For example, they might get a job selling cars and earn eighty thousand dollars a year in commissions. The young person then realizes that they are not as dumb as everyone said they were. They just have different gifts that were not being rewarded in school.

MANAGING WITH TEMPERAMENT

It is very important for managers to understand temperament. Without understanding temperament, it would be very easy for us to get the wrong person in the wrong job and blame the employee for their failure. Without understanding temperament, it would be very easy for managers to delegate the wrong work to the wrong employee. The key here is to find out what an employee's strengths are and help the employee use their strength for their job.

If you want to know if you or your employee is in the right job, just ask them if they get the "Sunday night blues." You know what I mean, it's Sunday night and you say to yourself, "I can't believe it's Sunday night, I don't want to get up in the morning and go to work." People who are in the right job for their gifts may not enjoy work some days but they definitely do not hate their job.

Before a friend of mine went to college, she was a legal secretary. She was very skilled at typing and could type ninety words a minute. The problem was that she got the Sunday night blues, the Monday night blues, the Tuesday night blues, the Wednesday night blues, and the Thursday night blues as well. She hated her job. Although she could do the job very well, because she did not like her job she was not very committed to the work. I encouraged her to seek her purpose in life. She decided to go to college, which was something she had always dreamed of doing but did not have the courage to do because she had a good paying job in the legal industry. Now she works in the social work field. She is an absolute star, she feels valuable to society, and she enjoys her work. My friend will tell you that one of the best days of her life was the day she graduated from college.

Say I am the CEO of the company. When I am putting together my top management team, I need to think about temperament. If I do what many top business leaders do, I would choose my management team based on how I feel about them and how I get along with them as well as the skills they list on their resumes and the work that they've done in the past. Using the style of hiring sometimes works but more often it does not. Generally, people are biased towards others that see the world as they do.

Say as CEO my temperament is director. Naturally, I will get along with other directors very well. I will be able to communicate with them easily and understand where they are coming from since their way of seeing the world is just like mine. If I hire like this I will probably get an unbalanced team. Because of my natural propensity towards other directors, I choose all directors for my management team. I probably think this is a great idea since I have chosen people who are just like me. When I make decisions is very easy to get consensus and everyone gets along.

The problem here is that the entire team sees the world from one perspective. The whole team is made of people who all desire to do important things. They all say, "Let's go to the moon." If the team had some detail people on the team, thinkers or relaters, they might tell us we have a large enough budget to get to the moon but we probably do not have enough to get back. You see it takes all types to create a solid team.

As CEO of a company, I want a socializer for vice president of marketing and sales. I want a thinker for vice president of research and development. I want a relater for vice president of human relations. I want a director for vice president of operations. When I build a team that is comprised all four temperaments, decisions made by the group will generally be very reliable. This concept is synergy. Synergy says that the sum is greater than the parts. One plus one equals more than two.

TEMPERAMENT AND COMMUNICATING

Every human being is born with a temperament, a genetic propensity to see the world in a certain way. The problem with communicating between temperaments is that some people never realized that others have different perspectives than they do. They live their lives with blinders on, thinking that they are always right and everyone else is wrong. The process of maturing in life generally helps people to take off the blinders and begin to respect other people's perspective.

When you get into an argument with somebody and they take an exact opposite position then you, you need to step back and look at the other perspective. If you take time to ask a person how they see the world, they can explain their point of view, and very quickly you will say, "I never even looked at it that way." In this way, we begin to respect the differences between the temperaments and realize that others have much to add to our perspective. As people begin to realize that others have different perspectives that are just as valid as their own, they begin to mature as human beings. This allows them to begin to take on aspects of other temperaments and become flexible in their thinking.

As we said earlier, people can bridge between two temperaments. Therefore, you can find people who are socializer-director, director-thinker, thinker-relater, or relater-socializer. What we do not naturally see occurring is relater-director, or thinker-socializer because these are opposite types. Have you ever gone on a trip and met someone new that you seem to understand as if you have known him or her for your whole life? Guess what, they are probably the same temperament as you. Did you ever go on a date with somebody that you were not able to communicate with very well? They were probably your opposite temperament.

Socializers and thinkers have opposite temperaments. Socializers are direct, open, and accepting. They love to talk and spend time with others. Thinkers are indirect, self-contained and assessing. They enjoy being alone where they can think. Can you see how they often do not communicate easily? They have very different ways of seeing the world.

Directors and relaters have opposite temperaments. Directors are direct, self-contained and assessing. They are very interested in success. At work that might say, "Let's shake things up a little bit here with some competition. That will make us all more productive." Relaters are indirect, open, and accepting. They are people oriented. Relaters say, "Why compete? Why don't we all cooperate instead, that will make us more productive?" These two types see the world from very different perspectives. The good news is that as people begin to respect the differences and understand temperament, they can synergize and utilize the strengths of each temperament.

RAISING CHILDREN USING TEMPERAMENT

Does anyone have a child that they think could not be from their genetic material? Many people do. For instance, you might have a child who is a thinker. If you are a socializer, you see the world painted with very broad strokes. You might tell your child, "This is the way the world works," using generalizations. Your thinker child might say, "What about this detail and what about that detail?" You probably see the forest and your child sees the trees.

Most of us raise our children to be exact clones of our selves. We often push our children to do the things that we enjoyed as children. It is very possible that your child will not like the things you enjoy because they experience the world from their own temperament not yours. You may love sports and social activities while your child enjoys spending time alone doing experiments and playing computer games.

What we need to do is change our approach towards our children. We need to stop trying to make them our clones and realize that they need to be respected according to their own temperament. For instance, talking to thinker children about science and math will be very interesting to them. Enrolling them in science camp is a good idea since they will probably find friends there who are just like them. We must realize how important it is for us to respect our children according to their own temperament. This makes a powerful point for management. We need to respect our employees according to their own temperaments. We need to put them in the right job and delegate work to them that is compatible with their temperament. In this way, we will maximize their strengths.

EMPLOYEES AND TEMPERAMENT

Say I have an employee who is a superstar salesperson but all of their paperwork is done sloppily because they do not spend time on the details. I can either say to that employee, "You bad employee I can't believe you are so lazy." or I can say, "I'm going to hire a relater who is good with details and paperwork. The relater is going to call you every day out in the field on your cell phone. You will give him your numbers verbally since this is the way you communicate best and the relater will fill in your forms for you. You're never going to have to do paperwork again."

With this action, do you think my salesperson is going to hate me? No, they will love me because I have taken away the thing that they hate to do and are not good at. I free them up to do what they love to do and are good at. I have also made their weakness irrelevant by building a team with complimentary or synergized temperaments. If you have the job description that says someone has to be great at communication skills and great at details, do you think that is a good job description? I suggest it is not. What you need to do is rewrite the job description to fit one temperament if possible.

If you have an employee who can do the job, but they hate the job, they will not be highly productive. I always say that I only want people working for me who love their job and are very good at it. If they do not love their job, or they are not good at it, I realize that they are not in the right job. Unfortunately, many people spend much of their life in the wrong job. They try very hard to succeed but they never quite get the hang of it and they blame themselves. The problem is not that they are not trying hard. The problem is that they are in the wrong job for their temperament.

Sometimes the best thing you can do with that employee who is not succeeding at work is to help them understand temperament. As they understand their strengths and weaknesses, they will begin to realize why they have not been successful at the job they have been doing. This will allow them to stop beating themselves up emotionally, and start to look for a job that fits their temperament. Where do most people spend most of their life? They spend it at work. If we keep someone in a job that they do not like or are not good at, are we doing them a favor? What we are really doing is co-depending with them and helping them waste their life.

In one of my seminars, a woman asked me, "Where were you when I got my divorce last year? As you were speaking, I just realized that I am a thinker and I was married to a socializer. I thought he was so dumb. He could not even balance the checkbook. I kept letting him know how dumb he was until one day he up and left me. Now I realize that he was very successful as a salesperson and made eighty thousand dollars a year. Maybe I should have balanced the checkbook and let him make the money and we would've made a good team."

This is the essence of building a good team. Building a team based on temperament will give you a balanced team that will anticipate problems before they get out of hand. Since team members all look at the problem from different perspectives, they will be able to avoid pitfalls.

5

OPTIMIZING PERFORMANCE SUCCESS

Have you ever wondered why some of your employees seem to take up a lot of your time? You work with these individuals repeatedly but they never seem to perform very well. They may be negative. They may be the kind of person that only works hard when you are looking over their shoulder. They may be the kind of person that never seems to be able to get to work on time. They may be the kind of person who does the minimum work and complains all the time that they should be paid more.

What we find is that the bottom ten percent of our employees creates fifty percent of our management headaches. If we can understand what is going on in the minds of these individuals, we can be much more successful as managers. Let us look at why some people are so successful naturally and why some people never seem to be able to get ahead.

One of the simplest things we have learned in studying human behavior is that the way we think in our minds determines how we approach work. We know that the way we feel about work determine the actions that we undertake during the day. Our actions create consequences and these consequences reinforce our original thoughts. We know that the way people think is determined originally by the way they have been socialized or brought up in childhood. At birth human beings have very little concept of how the world works. We watch how our parents and other authority figures act and interact with each other to understand how the world works. The way our parents interact and view the world creates our subconscious programming.

In some families, mom and dad come home from work and say things like, "I'm so excited about my work experience. We have such a great team at work and we are working on an important project that will really make the world a better place. I feel good about myself because I am successful at work. In addition, my boss told me that I am going to get a raise at the end of the year and be promoted to supervisor. Work is such a wonderful thing."

In that family when mom and dad get into a conflict they sit down at the kitchen table, talk it out, both sides compromise, and they respect each other. Learning from these parents gives the child a very positive way of seeing the world. Often these children will play at being a doctor, nurse, construction worker or some other kind of worker because mom and dad have promoted work as such a positive activity.

When the child becomes an adult and comes to work for you, the way they think about work the first day at work is that work is good. The way they think about work determines the way they act. People who believe that work is good generally will work very hard. I hope that their manager reinforces the positive behavior by praising the employee. The employee will feel respected for their contribution to the organization. This causes the original thought that work is good to be reinforced and causes the employee to work harder.

At the end of the year, the good employee might get further positive reinforcement in the form of a bonus or other positive recognition such as public praise at a company picnic or get-together. This further reinforces the original thought that work is good and causes the employee to work even harder. After several years of this positive behavior when there is an opportunity for promotion, generally the hard-working employee will be promoted. This further reinforces the positive behavior.

When this employee gets in an argument with somebody at work, what will they do? They follow their original training, talk it out, compromise, and respect the other person. They have great interpersonal communication skills without even having to try. If people have been programmed to look at work in a positive way in their childhood, their original subconscious programming sets them out on a path for success in their work environment. They have a gift from their parents that puts them on a trajectory straight up for success.

In other families, the parents give their children a very different way of seeing the world. In these families, mom or dad may come home from work and say things like, "Work is miserable. I cannot stand working for this company and I cannot stand working for my manager. We are so overworked and underpaid. No one respects me and I have been passed over for a promotion every year for the last 25 years. Life is just a cruel joke that is being played on me. I can't wait until I can finally retire and go fishing." The childhood training here is work is bad and fishing is good.

In this family, when mom and dad get into an argument they start screaming at each other. One spouse throws something across the room. The other spouse storms out of the house, slams the door, goes down to the bar, and gets drunk. They stay out until 3 a.m., come home and a few hours later get ready for work while still a little tipsy. Talk about childhood programming!

When this child grows up and comes to work for you, the way that they think about work the first day on the job is that work is bad. If they think that work is bad they do not work very hard. We do not praise them for not working hard. They say, "It's not fair, everyone else gets praised except for me." At the end of the year when it is time for bonuses, does this employee get a bonus? No. When it is time for somebody to be promoted, is this employee promoted? Not a chance. This employee says, "I'm treated so poorly here. I have been here 25 years and I have never been promoted. This company just has it out for me and my manager hates me." The truth is, it was the way the employee thought about work the first day on the job that determined how they were treated at work. When this employee gets in an argument with somebody at work, they start screaming and make a big fuss. Their childhood programming never prepared them to have good interpersonal relationships. This individual got a gift from their parents that set them out on a trajectory for failure.

This kind of simple training is easy to understand. However, some things happen in some people's childhoods that are incredibly damaging to their self-esteem. We all understand that people who have been abused or neglected in childhood will have psychological issues to deal with before they can live a full and happy life, but there are some hidden damagers of self-esteem. These hidden damagers of self-esteem are deeply embedded negative feelings in the individuals' subconscious that cause them to feel guilty or worthless.

Many people spend much of their life dealing with subconscious problems. Most of these people are never able to get past them because they do not even know what is holding them back. As a manager, it is imperative to understand the subconscious psychological problems that hold people back from achieving their full potential. Good managers are people who get the work done on time and on budget.

Great leaders are people who understand that their employees are their most valuable assets. They spend their time teaching, training, mentoring, and helping people maximize their human potential.

GUILT THROWING - GUILT CATCHING

Like most concepts in psychology, individuals learn how to feel about themselves early on in life. Parents do most of the training, and most parents train their children in exactly the same way they were trained. Unfortunately, many parents act in ways that can be very damaging to children. Naturally, each of our employees is just a grown-up child. Overriding feelings of guilt in the subconscious, or overriding feelings of worthlessness in the subconscious will have far-reaching effects that keep an individual from achieving their full potential. These are the hidden damagers of self-esteem.[5]

In many families, guilt is thrown around between spouses. Psychologists call it guilt-throwing and guilt-catching. One spouse is the guilt-thrower and the other

---

[5] Tracy (1984)

spouse is the guilt-catcher. If the wife is the guilt-thrower, in that household it may sound something like this. "I can't believe I married you. You are such a loser. You get a job and work for a short time but you always end up being fired. You come back here, sit on the couch, and drink beer all day. You get another job and you cannot hold that. I have to work two jobs just to pay the mortgage. You are dead weight. I should divorce you."

In that household, any time something goes wrong it is always the husband's fault. When the car breaks down the wife will say, "Why did you buy me that piece of junk at the buy-here pay-here lot? I told you to buy me a new car." Whenever something breaks down it is always the husband's fault. The husband is meek and mild, a guilt-catcher. He will say, "I'll work harder, I'll get a new job, you'll see, I'll take care of everything."

If it is the other way around and the husband is the guilt thrower it might very stereotypically sound something like this. "I can't believe I married you. You are so dumb you cannot even balance the checkbook. You never clean the house the way I like it. You never cook the food I like. On top of that, you are getting fat and ugly. I should divorce you." The wife is meek and mild, a guilt-catcher. She will say, "I'll work harder, I'll show you I can do things right. I'll get on an exercise program and I'll get some makeup."

While the parents are throwing guilt at each other, they have no idea that their children are watching and learning. Deep in their childhood programming, they are learning how to behave. Generally, the child will identify with one of the parents. They will model that parent's behavior and grow up to be a guilt-thrower or a guilt-catcher. Once they have grown up, they go out into the world and find their opposite, a guilt-thrower or a guilt-catcher, and get married. Then they have a bunch of babies who grow up to be guilt-throwers are guilt-catchers. And the cycle goes on from generation to generation but that is not a big problem.

The big problem is that it does not matter who they identify with. Deep in their subconscious programming, they know they are half of their mom and half of their dad. If dad was always so mean to mom and threw guilt at her all the time and mom never stood up for herself, children believe that mom must be guilty even though they are not sure what she did wrong.

The children will understand that since they are half of their mom and half of their dad and since mom was guilty, they must be guilty. They do not understand what mom did to deserve such treatment but they know she must have deserved it because she never stood up for herself. The child who grows up in a guilt throwing family has an overriding belief in their subconscious that they are also guilty even though they are not sure what they have done wrong.

When these individuals come to work for us, they are not highly productive. We know that high self-esteem in employees creates high productivity and low self-esteem can have a devastating impact on productivity. Naturally, an individual who has an overriding sense of guilt in their subconscious does not feel good about themselves and what is self-esteem but the way we see ourselves?

As managers, we try to help these people become more productive. We tell them, "If you work hard here all year you will get a bonus. If you work hard here for a few years you could even become a supervisor just like me." The individual's conscious mind says, "Wow, that's great. I cannot wait to get the bonus. I can't wait to become a manager." The problem is that their subconscious mind says, "You're guilty." What do you think guilty people believe they deserve in life, good things? No, they believe they deserve nothing at all or punishment since they are guilty people.

We try to motivate these individuals by telling them they will get good things in life. Unfortunately, since this does not fit in with their subconscious childhood programming, they cannot believe us. The more we try to motivate them by telling them that the result of good work is positive benefits, the worse they do as employees. We do not understand why we are not successful motivating these individuals because we do not understand what is going on in their subconscious minds. There is good news though, because knowledge of the problem is 98% of the solution. Most people spend their whole lives with no idea that childhood subconscious programming is holding them back. When they understand the cause of their problems, they can begin to walk away from low self-esteem.

WORTHLESSNESS

Worthlessness is another hidden destroyer of self-esteem. The easiest way for me to explain this to you is to give you two examples. These examples are gender-specific but do not get confused by the gender. These things happen to both women and men. The first example is Mary. Mary is a young girl in grade school. In her grade school, they decide they are going to have a cheerleading team. Mary is very excited and wants to try out for cheerleading. She comes home after school and says, "Mommy, Mommy, we're going to have a cheerleading team at school and I'm going to try out." Mary is the apple of Mommy's eye and Mommy loves Mary with all of her heart.

Mommy looks down at Mary and sees that Mary is a little bit chunky and not quite as pretty as all the other girls are. Mommy wants to protect Mary from getting her feelings hurt because she knows how cruel children can be. They will say exactly what is on their mind. So Mommy says to Mary, "Cheerleading is so dumb. Why don't we do an art project instead of the cheerleading? You are so good an art." However, Mary will not change her mind. She says, "I'm going to try out for cheerleading. I know I can do all those jumps and I saw the cheerleaders on television. Those cheerleaders are important people. I'm going to be a cheerleader."

Now Mommy is very scared for Mary since Mary will not change her mind. However, she knows she has a very powerful way to change Mary's mind that she learned early on when Mary was just a small child. Mary comes home from school the next day and says, "Mommy, will you play with me?" Mommy says, "No Mary, I don't have enough time. I have too much work to do to spend time with you." And she goes about her work. Mary tries to talk to Mommy, but Mommy gives her the cold shoulder and will not talk to Mary or spend any time with her because Mary will not obey Mommy.

This goes on for a day, two days, three days, four days and that is about all Mary can take. As a young girl, she needs Mommy's attention so she says to Mommy, "You're right Mommy, cheerleading is so dumb. Let's do the art project instead." Mommy is happy that Mary has chosen to obey her. She reaches down, gives Mary a big hug, and says, "Mary I love you so very much." She showers down all the affection Mary craves since Mary has decided to obey Mommy.

Mary is happy that Mommy is showing her attention but she learns right then that she is not lovable as a human being. Her behavior makes her lovable. When she obeys Mommy, Mommy loves her. When she does not obey Mommy, Mommy does not love her. Psychologists call this withholding love. Some of us may know it better as the silent treatment. This happens repeatedly throughout Mary's life.

She gets into middle school and wants to date that boy that Mommy does not like. Mary goes ahead and dates the boy, but Mommy withholds love and the relationship does not last. Mary graduates high school and wants to go across the country to college. Mommy does not think it is a good idea for her baby to be that far away from home so she withholds love. To win back her mother's love, Mary decides to go to the local community college or maybe she decides not to go to college at all. In Mary's subconscious a program starts. That program says, "I can't, I can't, I can't. I can't try anything risky or Mommy will withhold love."

Mary grows up and comes to work for you. You say to her, "Mary, will you learn the computer program? It sure would help out." And straight out of her subconscious and through her mouth comes two words, I can't. Here you have the classic underachiever. Mary will only do the minimum work to keep her job. She will never do anymore because she is afraid that if she tries to take on too much you, the authority figure, will not respect her.

Our second example is Mark. Mark is a boy whose father is a very powerful man in the community. He might be a doctor, a lawyer, or a politician. For our example, let us call him a neurosurgeon. He owns his own clinic, Neurosurgery Associates. He drives a Mercedes and lives in a big house. Everybody loves the great neurosurgeon because he saves so many lives. He gives to charity and is on the Board of Directors of many charitable organizations. Mark loves his daddy too. One day Mark comes home from school with a report card; five A's and one B. He is very excited and says, "Daddy, Daddy, look at my report card." The great man looks at the report card and says, "Why did you get the B? If you want to go to Harvard and be a great neurosurgeon like me, you have to get straight A's. Harvard Medical School only accepts top students." Daddy knows how to change Mark's behavior. He goes into his home office, closes the door, and withholds love from Mark. Mark is crushed.

Mark goes back to school and works very hard. One day he comes back with his report card, straight A's. He is so excited and says, Daddy, Daddy, I got straight

A's. Daddy says, "That's my boy. You're just like me, a chip off the old block." Daddy takes Mark down to the country club and tells everyone, that is my boy he is a genius. He is going to Harvard Medical School. He will be the next associate at Neurosurgery Associates. Mark is only 10 years old.

He learns right then that he is not lovable as a human being. It is his behavior that makes him lovable. When he is perfect, Daddy loves him. When he is less than perfect, Daddy does not love him. Mark learns that he must be perfect to earn his father's love. He goes back to school and graduates near the top of his class. He goes on to college and if he gets straight A's everything is fine. If he gets a C or a D, he might even drop out of college and start self-medicating his feelings of being a failure with drugs and alcohol.

A program has been built into Mark's subconscious. It says, "I must, I must, I must, I must be perfect." Mark grows up and comes to work for you. He is the kind of person who does five hours' worth of work in three hours and then walks around complaining that no one does any work but him. Sometimes we overlook his behavior and promote Mark higher and higher in the organization because he is such a good worker. When Mark becomes president of the organization and when there is a problem, does he take personal responsibility? How can he take personal responsibility if he believes he must be perfect? He cannot, so he blames others for the problem.

How about when things go right in the organization? Maybe you have created great success in your unit and increase profits by twenty percent for the organization. You go to Mark and tell him about your success. He goes to the owners of the Company, and what does he do? He takes personal credit for your work.

Whenever you talk to Mark, he always tells you about his personal achievements, the big new house he is building, and the expensive new car he is going to buy. He always seems to be bragging about himself. The truth is, he is propping up his feelings of worthlessness with achievements and possessions. Down deep inside

Mark knows that he is not perfect and he feels worthless.

We understand how damaging withholding love is in a young person's life because there have several studies done at orphanages. In one orphanage, they put babies in cribs, changed their diapers, and fed them. They did not hug them, sing to them, or give them any affection. About one third of the babies stopped eating, physically dried up, and died. In another orphanage, children who were not given proper love grew up to have extremely low IQs of between 50 and 100. Other studies showed that babies in orphanages who were not nurtured had sunken appearances and lay so long in a fixed position that they lost the ability to turn over and look around. Human beings need unconditional love as much as they need air, water, and food to survive.

FIXING THE PROBLEM

Much research has been done on why some people are successful in life and why others struggle just to keep a job. The one thing that all of these people have in common is low self-esteem based on inadequate socialization in childhood. It has been well documented that child neglect of all kinds is very damaging to children. It is also clear that the hidden damagers of self-esteem that cause guilt and worthlessness affect huge amounts of the population and hold them back from a living a full, happy and successful life.

If you want to find out if one of your employees is suffering from low self-esteem just ask them a simple question. Do not do it as manager to employee, but rather as person-to-person over lunch. Tell them a little bit about your childhood and then ask them how they grew up. If they had one of these things happen to them in their childhood and they are willing to share with you, one, two, or three sentences will come out of their mouth very quickly.

The first sentence would be, "My dad was so mean to my mom all the time." If this sentence comes out of their mouth, you know they are suffering from an overriding sense of guilt in their subconscious. If they say, "My mommy was overprotective and would never let me do any of the things I wanted to do." You know they are suffering from a sense of worthlessness that causes them to be underachievers. If they say, "I could never be good enough to please my daddy." You know they are suffering from a sense of worthlessness that causes them to be over achievers. (Obviously, they could say mommy, daddy, or both in any of the sentences.) Once we have diagnosed the problem, what do we do?

There are many forms of therapy that can help individuals get past their childhood programming, but there is one very powerful form of therapy to help people get over guilt and worthlessness. This therapy is called Rational Emotive Behavior Therapy (REBT).[6] It is a very powerful way to change childhood programming and it costs nothing because we can often do it by ourselves.[7]

---

[6] Ellis & Ellis (2011)

[7] This information is given for informational purposes only. If you feel you need psychological assistance, please contact your Employee Assistance Program or a licensed psychologist.

The concept is that we must rationally debate irrational beliefs. If I was to believe that I was guilty when I had done nothing wrong, would that be rational? Obviously, it would not. Therefore, what I need to do is to rationally debate the irrational belief whenever it comes into my mind. Whenever I feel guilty, I must use my conscious mind and say to myself, "Why do I feel guilty? I haven't anything wrong, therefore I am not guilty, and I will not feel guilty any longer." Psychologists have found that when we rationally debate irrational beliefs, the old believe will begin to go away and it will be replaced by the new belief.

If the feeling comes in my mind that I cannot do something I must ask myself why I feel that I cannot do that thing. I must tell myself that the reason I feel I cannot achieve it is only because love was withheld in my childhood to keep me from trying risky things. I must tell myself, "I can do that. I can achieve it and therefore I will try."

If the feeling comes into my mind that I must be perfect, I need to tell myself that the reason I feel this way is because love was withheld to make me an overachiever. I must tell myself that I do not have to be perfect. "I'm a normal person. Sometimes I am successful and sometimes I make mistakes. When I make mistakes, I learned from my mistakes and that is a good thing. I'm not a hero and I'm not a zero and that is okay."

The reason rational emotive behavior therapy works is because of how the brain works. Recent neurological studies have discovered the fact that the brain is what we call a neural network. The brain cells that contain our memories, ideas, concepts, and beliefs are connected to each other through neural wiring. The neural wiring can be strengthened or a weakened over time. "When we practice an action such as riding a bike or playing the piano or studying for the SATs, the connections between brain cells called synapses become stronger. Connections that do not get used eventually dwindle and disappear."[8] Your brain is essentially a map of your worldview. As your worldview changes so does the internal map that is your brain.

[8] Nedivi (2000)

Since we may have some memories that hold us back, we must change those memories. What we find is that memories that we use all the time become very easy for us to access. Memories that we do not use very often become harder for us to access. This is because the more you use a memory, the stronger the neural connection to that part of your brain becomes.

With rational emotive behavior therapy, we are simply strengthening the connection to the new memory, idea or thought pattern, while weakening the connection to the old memory by not using it. We all know the old saying, "If you don't use it you will lose it." That saying is true. The fact is that some memories do not help us. The memories that hold us back must be weakened while new, positive memories and thought patterns must be built to replace the old negative thought patterns. Researchers tell us that within thirty to forty five days of rationally debating irrational beliefs, the old memories begin to fade and new thought patterns begin to take over. In this way, we can reprogram our minds for success.

6

MORAL REASONING

Many times managers who understand new management theory and practice the art of employee empowerment still do not get the productivity gains they are looking for with certain individuals. Often this is because the employee does not have the level of emotional maturity or moral reasoning that allows them to succeed in an empowerment environment. To better understand this phenomenon, we need to look at Kohlberg's levels of moral reasoning.[9]

From Lawrence Kohlberg's research, we know that individuals move through six distinct levels of moral

---

[9] Kohlberg (1981)

reasoning. I have modified Kohlberg's concepts somewhat to make the concepts easier to apply for managers.

I call level one: Me-Me-Me. This is childlike reasoning. Individuals at level one seek to fulfill their desires at any cost to others. When a child is born, they naturally have needs that others must fulfill. As they grow up, they maintain this childlike reasoning until a negative consequence teaches them to behave in more mature ways.

If you take a very young child into a candy store, the child will look around and say, "I want some candy." Sometimes the child will take the candy without any thought that it is not their candy. They do not understand the concept of private property and they are only concerned with the filling their desire at that moment. Hopefully, at that point Mom or Dad says to the child, "That is not your candy. Please say sorry to the owner of the store. We will have to pay for the candy and you will have timeout when we get home."

The timeout is a negative consequence designed to teach the child that they must change their behavior.

Since people do not like negative consequences, most children quickly learn to modify their behavior to avoid the negative consequence. After several timeouts, they may think to themselves, "I don't like timeouts. How can I change my behavior so as to avoid the timeout?" At that point, they may ask their parent, "Can I have some money to buy some candy?" Often the parent will say something like, "If you clean your room, I'll give you the money to buy some candy." The child learns that they can bargain for the money and thereby avoid the negative consequence. This moves them to level two.

I call level two: Bargaining. At level two, the individual believes that the way to fill their desires is through bargaining. "I'll scratch your back if you scratch my back." At this level, the individual will only do something for someone else if they are guaranteed a return on investment. Bargaining may work quite well for the child until they get in a social environment like kindergarten where norms are enforced through peer pressure. Here the child learns that they will be excluded if they do not fit in with the dominant group and they do not have enough resources to bargain with the entire group for acceptance. They learn to avoid negative consequences by following group norms. This moves them to level three.

I call level three: Peer-Pressure. At level three, the individual becomes concerned with fitting in to a group. There are socially accepted ways of behaving that an individual must conform to so as not to be ostracized. To avoid the negative consequence of being excluded from the group, the individual modifies their behavior and follows group norms. Peer pressure works quite well most of the time, but occasionally it can cause problems. Say the young person gets a car and their driving license. They are driving around with their friends on a Friday evening and their friend say, "How fast can this car go?" The young person bows to peer-pressure and puts the pedal to the metal. The police catch them and give them a speeding ticket. The young person learns that to avoid the negative consequence of speeding tickets they must obey the law of the land. This moves them to level four.

I call level four: Law of the Land. At level four, what is legal is what is right, so the individual follows the law of the land. Many people spend their entire lives at level four. Some people move on to higher levels moral reasoning through education, philosophy, and religion. They realize that blindly following the law of the land now and again creates injustice. To solve this dilemma they must move to an abstract understanding of reality. This moves them to level five.

I call level five: Abstract Reasoning. At level five, the individual realizes that occasionally laws, taken literally, will conflict with what is best for human beings. At this level, the individual realizes that laws were created to serve humans and not the other way around. For example, if my wife is labor and about to have a child, I need to get her in the car and drive as fast as is reasonably safe to the hospital to make sure she gets there in time. If a police officer pulls me over and I explain the situation, the officer will probably help me break more laws like running stoplights and stop signs as I follow her to the hospital. The officer realizes that the wellbeing of my wife and unborn child are more important than the traffic laws.

I sometimes call level five, "What goes around comes around." People at level five of emotional maturity realize that in this cosmic reality, the way they treat others affects how they are treated. When they treat people poorly, they end up getting negative returns for their negative social investment over time. When they treat people respectfully, they end up getting positive returns on their positive social investment over time. As people learn to avoid the negative consequences that inevitability flow from poor social behavior, they move on to level six.

I call level six: Altruism. At level six, the individual does kind things for others without any desire for personal gain. An individual at level six might give to charity without interest in recognition. A level six billionaire might build a free hospital for the poor and not want their name inscribed in stone above the entryway. Very few people have the ability to live at level six continuously. Most people who achieve level six bounce back and forth between level five and level six. Occasionally they might even get mad at someone, slip to level one, and do something mean. When they do slip, they apologize for their actions and return to bouncing between level five and level six.

It is very important for managers to understand Kohlberg's levels of moral reasoning. Many times managers who are at level five or level six of moral reasoning are dealing with employees who are at level one or level two. Kohlberg tells us that individuals move sequentially through the six levels of moral reasoning and cannot understand more than one level of moral reasoning above the level they are at. Kohlberg also tells us that individuals will not move to higher levels of moral reasoning without some form of negative consequence that unveil the flaws in their current reasoning. Because managers do not understand this, they communicate using higher levels of moral reasoning and very wrongly believe that the level one employee will understand level five or level six moral reasoning.

They treat the employee with respect, give the employee the benefit of the doubt, and expect the employee to reciprocate in the relationship. An employee at level one will say to himself, "My manager is very easy to take advantage of. I can do whatever I want and she will accept any excuse I give her." Like a very young child, the level one individual only respects rewards and punishment. Therefore, they will only work hard when we offer them a reward or they fear punishment. Unfortunately, this is what hierarchical management style is based upon. The problem with hierarchical management, as we stated earlier, is that when we are not watching employee they will take advantage of us because hierarchical management style creates an "us-versus-them" environment. Management is seen as the enemy and the goal of the employee is to do the least amount of work for the most amount of pay.

As managers, we have to differentiate between employees who have achieved higher levels of moral reasoning and those that do not. We cannot deal with individuals at very low levels of moral reasoning as we would those at higher levels of moral reasoning because Kohlberg shows us that individuals can only understand one level of moral reasoning higher than the level they are on at any point in time. When we treat individuals who are on a low level of moral reasoning as if they were at high levels of moral reasoning, we will not achieve the desired results. This is one of the things that confuse managers who seek to introduce new management theory in the work environment.

How can you know what level of emotional maturity your employee is at? At level one of moral reasoning, when you asked the employee to help someone they will generally say, "What's in it for me?" Remember, level one is all about me-me-me. At level two of moral reasoning, when you asked the employee to help someone they will generally say, "How much will you pay me?" People at level two of moral reasoning are always bargaining. You try to explain to the level one or level two employee that they should just help because it is the right thing to do. They look at you as if you are out of your mind. Why would they do something for someone else without some kind of return for themselves? They cannot understand level five or level six moral reasoning.

With employees at very low levels of moral reasoning, we may need to use discipline to help the employee move to higher forms of moral reasoning. Since we know that individuals will not move to higher levels of moral reasoning without some form of negative consequence that unveil the flaws in their current reasoning, discipline can provide the motivation for individuals to move to higher levels of moral reasoning. When I speak of discipline, I am not talking about punishment or revenge. Discipline is a very positive action meant to help an individual move to higher levels of moral reasoning. It is done out of concern for the individual and never done out of anger or for revenge.

Much like a child's timeout, the traditional discipline process of verbal warning, written warning, day of suspension and finally termination creates the environment that often helps individuals change their way of interacting with others and helps them move to higher levels of moral reasoning. When individuals respond to the discipline process and change their behavior they should be rewarded with praise and other positive encouragement that reinforces the new behavior.

As a manager, you will have success with employees who are at least at level three of emotional maturity. At level three of emotional maturity, peer-pressure, employees want to be accepted as a part of the group and therefore they will follow group norms and expectations. At level four, the employee will also follow the laws of the land. At level five, the employee realizes through abstract reasoning that what goes around comes around. They will do their work even when you are not there to supervise because they know that the world works best when we fulfill our obligations. Most level six employees will be found in very high positions in the organization that is as it should be. They understand that true leadership is serving others altruistically.

Occasionally, people with low levels of emotional maturity will achieve positions of power. They generally achieve their position through bullying and by using fear as a motivator. This hierarchical management style creates the "us versus them" atmosphere in an organization. Leaders who use the hierarchical management style are looking out for number one. They will always put their own interests above the interests of other stakeholders in the organization including employees, other managers, the board of directors and stockholders.

7

DELEGATION

From our discussion on temperament, we know that building a team that includes all four temperaments generally gives us the best results. Once we have built our team we have to understand how to maximize the performance of the individuals in the team. Delegation is a key to building successful teams. What we do is delegate work to the individual that is just a little more difficult and the work they are doing right now. Once they learn a new skill, their sense of competence goes up. A greater sense of competence increases self-esteem and we know that high self-esteem employees are highly productive employees.

Let us say that I am the president of an organization and I need to promote one of my managers. I have two candidates to choose from. Both candidates are great managers in that they both get the work done on time and on budget. One manager sees their job as more than getting the work done on time and on budget. They believe that they have a responsibility to teach, train and mentor the people they manage. This manager has chosen one outstanding individual and has trained that individual on every aspect of the manager's job. The other manager does not teach, train, or mentor. Which manager do I promote and why? If I promote the manager who does not teach, train, or mentor, either I will have to hire his or her replacement at high cost outside the organization or I will have to train the new manager internally. This will take up my time and the new manager will not be up to speed for several months. If you are not training one individual on every aspect of your job now, are you preparing yourself for a promotion?

If I promote the manager who does the teaching, training, and mentoring, I will have an already trained replacement for his or her position. Very pragmatically, I will always choose to promote the individual who is a teacher, trainer, and mentor. Not only do they have a replacement ready, they are also truly great leaders. Great leaders are those that see the individuals that they manage as important assets that need to be developed.

There are many reasons that people choose not to do delegation. Some of them might be fear that they will lose control, the fact that they do not trust their people, the idea that if you want something done right you should do-it-yourself, and many more. These are all delegation traps. As managers, we must learn to delegate. Managers should think of the work that they do day-to-day and divide it into neck-up work and neck-down work. Neck-down work is generally physical in nature. Neck-up work is mental in nature and includes all of the traditional management duties of planning, organizing, delegating, training, teaching, and mentoring. Great managers delegate neck-down work. Great leaders delegate neck-up work. In delegating neck-up work, they build new leaders who can handle management responsibilities. This expands the value of the organization.

We know that our people are the only appreciating assets in business. If you own a building, you must continually do upkeep. While the land it is built on might appreciate or depreciate, the building will depreciate unless it is maintained. If your company owns equipment, the equipment will depreciate over time. As we teach our employees new skills and build their sense of competence, they appreciate and become much more valuable to us.

Some people do not like to delegate. They know that if they are the only ones who know how to do something at work they cannot be fired and they enjoy having that feeling of job security. The problem here is that if you cannot be fired, there are several other things that cannot happen for you as well. How about going on vacation? One manager came into my seminar very upset. She had just come back from vacation and her boss had called her three times a day on her cell phone on the beach. I told her, "It sounds like you had a working vacation." I asked her if there was anything at work that only she knew how to do. She admitted that there was. I told her, "The next time you go on vacation make sure you have trained at least one individual on every single aspect of your job."

If you do not train people on every aspect of your job, it is probably very difficult for you to go on vacation.

How about getting sick? You get sick and you are in the hospital. The boss calls you in the hospital and says, "It's Friday and we don't know how to do payroll." You say, "Bring the laptop to my hospital room and I'll do the payroll."

I had another manager come into my seminar extremely distraught. She managed an engineering firm where ten engineers would go through a process every day. The lead engineer who had been at the firm for many years, got burned out and started not to show up for work. When that engineer was out no one could get any work done because the lead engineer was the only one who understood how to do the initial step of the process. Whenever the lead engineer did not come to work, the manager had nine expensive engineers with nothing to do. I told her that there was not much that could be done at that point except for training an engineer on the initial step. The advice I gave her was to cross train all of her engineers on at least two tasks so that when one was absent she would have a backup.

I had one manager in my seminar that was certain that filing papers was part of her management job. I asked her what her boss thought about that. She said that the boss did not think she should be doing the filing and that was the reason he sent her to the seminar. We talked a little while and the manager told me that the reason she does the filing is to prove to her employees that she is not above them. I told her that was admirable in theory, but then I asked her if she was being paid more than her employees were paid. She admitted that she was. I asked her if it was more cost effective for her to do the filing or for her employees to do the filing. She realized that it was more cost effective to have the employees do the filing and for her to spend her time doing neck-up work. It's okay for a manager to jump in and helped employees do their work occasionally to show solidarity or to pick up the slack when there's too much work to do, but in general duties should be delegated to the lowest level that can do them.

Many managers come into my seminars expressing that they cannot delegate certain very detail oriented and important tasks because they are afraid they will not be done correctly. If this is a case, I suggest you hire your clone. I am certain that there is an individual out there is just as detail oriented as you are. Hire someone who is just like you and delegate that work.

Some people believe it is easier to do the work themselves because it takes more time to teach someone how to do it then to do it yourself. This is a very shortsighted view since although it may take some time to teach the individual, once they have learned you never have teach them again. Over the long run, you gain efficiency because the individual knows how to do the job. As a manager if you are spending more than forty hours consistently at work, either you are short staffed or you have not mastered the skill of delegation.

8

MISTAKES

When Thomas Edison was inventing the light bulb, he failed approximately nine thousand times. One person asked him why he continued to try to invent the light bulb after so much failure. Edison's response was that he had never failed at all. Nine thousand times he had learned how not to make a light bulb. Edison saw mistakes for their true value, the opportunity to learn.

The quality of a manager can easily be determined by viewing how they deal with problems. Competent managers see problems as a challenge. They do not seek to avoid problems but instead they diligently seek to find problem areas on their own. When problems are found they analyze the problem, search for the best solution and quickly move to correct problems before they get out of hand. They have confidence in their problem-solving abilities and they are able to make decisions quickly after analyzing risks and benefits. They are willing to take calculated risks and they appreciate that mistakes are excellent opportunities for learning both for themselves and for employees.

Some managers avoid any risk because they fear making mistakes. If we avoid all risk, we will not achieve much success. We all know the old saying; no risk no reward. When managers make mistakes, they cannot beat themselves up emotionally. If I make a big mistake at work and lose the company ten thousand dollars, what I need to do is to come to work the next day and try to mitigate the damage to the best of my ability.

After dealing with the problem to the best of my ability, I need to learn as much as I can from the mistake and then forget about it. If I obsess over the fact that I made a mistake, the next time I must make a big decision will I trust myself? No, I will think to myself,

"The last time I made a big decision it didn't turn out well, how can I trust myself to make another decision?" As a manager I must trust my own decision making abilities if I want to be successful.

After talking with and teaching hundreds of entrepreneurs, I have learned that they all have one thing in common; they have all made some big mistakes. Many of them have filed bankruptcy but they did not give up. They learned from that mistakes and used what they had learned to make them successful in their new endeavors. Walt Disney was broke several times and even filed bankruptcy before he was successful with The Walt Disney Company. It is a good thing he did not give up or we would not have Disney Land, Disney World, Epcot Center and all the wonderful Disney movies and cartoons that we enjoy.

Once we realize that we are normal humans that make mistakes, and we are willing to learn from those mistakes instead of beating ourselves up emotionally, we must also realize that our employees are humans too and that they will make mistakes. When our employees make mistakes, we must allow them to learn from those mistakes instead of beating them down verbally. Say you have an employee, John, who makes a big mistake. What you need to say is, "John we didn't get the results we were looking for. What can we learn from this? What can we do differently next time to have better success?" Let John explain what he has learned and what he needs to modify to be more successful and then delegate the same work to John.

We know the old saying that when you are thrown from a horse what you must do is get back on. This concept applies to work. When John makes a mistake, he must be given the opportunity to learn from that mistake and try repeatedly until he is successful. When John finally learns how to do the task he will feel more competent because learning a new task always increases in individual's sense of competence. As competence increases, self-esteem increases and productivity increases as well. Once we understand this, we realize that mistakes can be turned into opportunities for productivity gains.

9

ASSERTIVENESS

I believe that the beginning of real success in management as well as in life starts by saying three simple words: I am responsible. I am responsible for my life and everything that happens in my life. I am also responsible for everything that happens in the unit I am managing. So when things go wrong in my unit is it because of all of those lazy employees? Some managers say, "If only I had some better employees my unit would be so much more successful." Saying this means we are not taking responsibility. As managers, we must take responsibility for everything that happens in our unit.

Say for instance, I have the meanest boss on the planet. He or she is a tyrant, vindictive, mean, and difficult to work for. If I say, "I am a victim of this mean boss," am I taking personal responsibility for my own life? No, I have to realize that I have a choice. On one hand, if I believe that I can help the boss change over time I may decide to stay at my job. However, if I do not believe that the boss will ever change then I must get out my résumé and get another job. If I stay in a relationship where I am being victimized I have only myself to blame.

Many people do not take personal responsibility because it is much easier to blame others. To better understand how to take control of one's own life, we need to look at assertive behavior. The definition of assertive behavior is standing up for one's own rights while respecting the rights of others. Let us look at the other kinds of behavior before we talk further about assertive behavior. There are four types of behavior, aggressive, passive, passive-aggressive, and assertive.

An example of aggressive behavior would be that we realize that our organization is being mismanaged so we go back to the boss and start yelling at the boss. We tell the boss that he or she is incompetent. Clearly, this aggressive behavior could very well lead to us being fired. We cannot be aggressive.

An example of passive behavior would be that we realize that our organization is being mismanaged so we go back to work and do not say a word because we do not want to rock the boat. Is passive behavior okay for managers? Of course not, we are paid to be problem solvers and passive behavior never creates successful organizations.

An example of passive-aggressive behavior is an employee who is nice to you when you are in their presence but behind your back, they say bad things about you. They tell you how wonderful a manager you are and how they enjoy working for you and all the while they are writing down everything you do wrong with the intent to pass it on to your boss and try to get you fired. They are nice to your face and stab you in the back.

Passive aggressive people are the most dangerous people in a work environment but how do you know who the passive aggressive individuals are? It is quite simple to know who the passive aggressive individuals are. They are the ones who show up at your office all the time telling you what everyone else is doing. You may think they are valuable because they are your spy. The truth is they are stabbing everyone in the back.

When you are not there, whom else do you think they are stabbing in the back? Yes, you are the number one target. These people have their nose in everyone's business. They are always gossiping. When you are not around, whom do you think they are gossiping about? They are gossiping about you. These people do not change their behavior. If they are back stabbers and gossips with others, they will stab you in the back and gossip about you behind your back.

Passive aggressive people destroy the sense of community in your organization. We know that if we lower the sense of community we lower the self-esteem of the individuals inside the organization and productivity will decrease. Our job as managers is to increase productivity. Passive-aggressive people are working against us. When I encounter a passive-aggressive person in my organization, I will stop the behavior immediately. When passive-aggressive are gossiping about others, what are they not doing? They are not working.

What I will do to stop the passive-aggressive behavior is to tie the behavior to productivity. I will get the passive-aggressive individual in my office and tell them, "I have noticed you are spending a lot of time gossiping. I am paying you to work not to gossip. This is your verbal warning. The next time I catch you gossiping instead of working I will give you a written warning. If I catch you gossiping and not working a second time, I will give you a day off to think if you want to continue working here or not. The third time I catch you gossiping instead of working you will be terminated."

I will also tie their passive-aggressive behavior to the productivity of others. We know that their passive aggressive-behavior destroys the sense of community. Lowering the sense of community reduces productivity and therefore I will document how other people view the passive-aggressive person and how their behavior reduces the team's productivity.

The only behavior style that works at work as well as in life is assertive behavior. Say that I have a mean, vindictive boss. I go to work and my self-esteem is at level eight out of ten. My boss yells at me all day and calls me incompetent. By the time I go home my self-esteem is at level two. Who is responsible? I am responsible. Either I must confront the boss in a respectful way to get the boss to change his or her behavior, or I must get out my résumé and get a new job. To stay in a victimizing situation is passive behavior. If I am being victimized, ultimately it is my fault because I stay in proximity to the victimizer.

I am not saying that assertive behavior is always easy. When we confront the boss with their negative behavior, there is great risk. Some low self-esteem individuals hate to have their employees hold up a mirror and show them their bad behavior. Because of this, many managers are afraid to confront the boss. The problem with passive behavior is that it always ends up in aggressive behavior. If you do not confront the boss and just take the abuse, you will bottle up your anger inside until it finally explodes out of you in the form of physical or verbal aggression. Generally, the people we will take out our anger and frustration on are our family and friends. Is this fair to them? Of course not. We must learn assertive behavior so we will not become aggressive abusers ourselves.

If we go to the boss and confront them with their abusive behavior in a respectful manner, are we standing up for our own rights? Yes, we are. When we confront the boss about their abusive behavior in a respectful way, are we respecting the boss's rights? Yes we are. If we do not stand up for our own rights who will? No one will. Anytime we do not stand up for our own rights while respecting the rights of others, we are not being assertive. Assertive behavior is the only behavior that works.

As I said before, assertive behavior is not without risks. When confronted with his or her own bad behavior, a low self-esteem boss may become angry and even more vindictive. More often than not though, when confronted with their bad behavior, victimizers will move on to weaker prey because bullies generally pick on the weak. I have taught thousands of managers from hundreds of companies and most of them agree that when they are assertive bully bosses move on and pick on other weaker passive individuals. There is sometimes risk in assertive behavior, but the risk of passive behavior, which always results in aggressive behavior, is far greater. No manager will ever become highly successful over the long run if they do not learn assertive behavior.

10

HIRING THE RIGHT PEOPLE

In my seminars I always say, "Hire the right people in the first place and many of your headaches will go away." However, how do we know how to hire the right people? It is actually simpler than one might expect. Obviously, we need people that are positive, enthusiastic, self-starters, and are hard workers. However, you also need people who fit the job temperamentally. When you are interviewing an individual, there are several things you can do to get better results from your hiring practices.

To find out if an individual is positive look for them saying things like, "I can" and "I will" a lot. What you want to avoid is individuals who say, "I can't" and "I won't" or "I'll try." When an individual says, "I'll try," I will immediately clarify and asked them, "Will you or won't you? I need someone who will commit to doing the job." If the person continues to say, "I'll try," or "I'll give it my best shot," or "I'll do my best," I will not hire that individual. If the person clarifies and says, "Yes I will do it." Then I might hire the individual. When I hear, "I'll try," I hear an individual giving himself or herself an out. If they do not succeed they can always say, "I tried." I would rather an individual who commits to doing the job unequivocally and fails then an individual who does not commit.

To find out if an individual is enthusiastic I simply ask them, "How do you feel about coming to work for me?" You can hear enthusiasm in the voice. They might say something like, "I have been waiting for a long time for this opportunity to come to work at this organization." Now they may be exaggerating, but at least they are exaggerating enthusiastically.

To find out if an individual is a self-starter I asked them, "What have you done in the last six months to make yourself a better person?" What I am looking for here is a person who says things like, "I learned auto mechanics," "I took a class," "I read a book," or "I went to a seminar," etc. People who are always looking for ways to improve themselves are self-starters. They are the people in your organization who see a problem and fix it before they have to be told.

To find out if someone is going to be a hard worker I ask him or her, "Do you have any hobbies? I do not really care what the answer is as long as it is something positive. The answer could be, "I coach soccer," "I go rock climbing," "I play guitar," "I do needlepoint," "I work on hot rods," etc. What I do not want to hear is, "I've got this wonderful recliner at home with a six-pack cooler built into the arm. I go home, crack a brew, recline, and watch my one hundred channels of sports on satellite television. I've been through three remotes in the last six months." This is what I call recliner level energy. I think we all know the old saying, "If you want to get something done ask a busy person."

A person who spends all of their free time reclining will often come to work and recline on my time.

Once I find an individual who is positive, enthusiastic, a self-starter, and a hard worker, I also need to know if they are going to fit into the specific job I am hiring for. The way I do this is I think of the person in my organization that is doing the job the best. I will write down all of the skills and traits this individual has on a piece of paper. I will photocopy the paper and keep a copy in front of me when I am interviewing individuals. As I interview, I will check off all the skills and traits the individual has. After I am done with the interviewing process, I will hire the individual who has the most skills and traits of the individual who is doing the job best in my organization. I know I have the right fit when I find a person who is positive, enthusiastic, a self-starter, a hard worker and they have the right skills, traits and temperament.

If you do not have someone in your organization is already doing the job, do not worry, just write down all the skills and traits you believe an individual needs to achieve success and hire on that basis. If you have a job that you would like to delegate but you do not feel comfortable delegating that duty because you do not have an individual who is as conscientious and detail oriented as you are, just hire your clone. Write down all the skills and traits that you have and hire an individual who is just like you. I guarantee there is someone out there who is just as conscientious and detail oriented as you are. With these simple skills, you will be able to hire much better people.

11

SYSTEM PROBLEMS

The Gallup organization did an extremely large poll to find out what made some managers very successful and some managers are not successful. They polled ten million customers, one million employees, and two hundred thousand managers.[10] What they found is that the greatest managers spend time one-on-one with their employees getting to know them. They create an environment where there is high trust between manager and employee.

Good managers spend a lot of time thinking about how they can increase the productivity of their employees.

---

[10] Buckingham & Coffman (1999)

They spend time one-on-one with the employee asking them questions about how the organization can help them be more successful in their work. Great managers take time to get feedback from their employees. They give each employee at least fifteen or twenty minutes of time every quarter to express their concerns. During this time, the employee has the opportunity to let the manager know where the problems are in the organization and what can be done to remedy the problems.

If during this one-on-one time the employee does not feel comfortable opening up to the manager, the manager must ask open-ended questions to get the employee to share. Here are some of the examples of questions managers should ask. "How can we as an organization be more successful? How can I as a manager help you be more successful at you work? Are there any things that we as an organization are doing that hold you back from being fully productive? How can we get you to be more committed to this organization? How can I make your job easier for you to perform?" If we ask these kinds of questions employees will give us feedback. The feedback will not always be what we expect.

If we take time to listen to our employees, we will find out what is holding our employees back from being highly productive. Most top managers take this one-step further and ask employees to fill out reverse evaluations. A reverse evaluation is where the employee evaluates the manager. This should be done anonymously. Put a box in the break room where employees can deposit the evaluations. The first time you do a reverse evaluation you will find out a whole lot about how good a manager you are from the perspective of your employees. The reverse evaluation helps us realize what we are doing right and what things we need to improve on. It gives us the knowledge we need to create a better sense of community for our employees. It also shows employees that we care about how they perceive their work environment.

Poor managers do not take time to evaluate the work environment. They immediately assume that the employees cause all of the problems. Researchers who analyze work environments show us that this is generally not the case. In fact, the rule of thumb is that eighty percent of problems in organizations are created by system problems. System problems are problems in the way the business is being run. Employees create only twenty percent of the problems in organizations. To find out if you have a system problem or a people problem is very simple. All you have to do is ask your people. If more than twenty percent of your people are complaining about something, you have a system problem. If less than twenty percent of your people complain it is probably a problem with those individuals.

System problems can be as simple as using the hierarchical management style instead of new management theory, not having written job descriptions to clarify expectations, having over burdensome rules and procedures that get in the way of productivity, having inadequate equipment, and many more. However, there is one major system problem that I believe over fifty percent of organizations in the United States have in common. I believe that this main system problem creates more negativity and lowers productivity more than all of the other system problems combined. Because of this, I want to take some time discussing it so that we will never allow the system problem to destroy our organizations. To illustrate this system problem I would like to tell you a story. It is a time-tested story that many management experts tell.

12

THE GOLDEN EGG

A farmer is down on his luck. The crops did not come in. The mortgage is due for that month on the farm and he does not have any money. He only has a few scraps of bread left to eat and he does not know how he will be able to buy more food. He is very worried. He goes out into the barnyard and he sees his last, favorite goose. He goes over to the goose and says, "Goose, goose, what am I going to do? I am going to starve. I'm going to lose the farm." The goose makes a lot of noise and jumps off the nest. The farmer reaches down in the nest to see if he can find an egg. He finds an egg and pulls it out of the nest. However, this egg is hard as rock. It is extremely heavy and off-color. The farmer is so angry that he throws the egg into the garbage. He shouts at the goose, "Don't you know that I am hungry? I cannot believe you laid that rotten egg. You knew I needed something to eat." The farmer stomps off into the farmhouse.

A couple days pass and the farmer is getting extremely hungry because he has finished off all of the scraps of bread. He is getting severe hunger pains and the hunger pains are causing him to think some crazy thoughts. He starts to think, that the egg was hard and heavy and off-color. It had a golden hue. Maybe it was made of gold. He rushes out into the barnyard and routs through the trash to find the egg. Once he finds the egg, he takes it down to a jeweler and asks him, "I know this sounds crazy but could this egg be made out of gold?" The jeweler tests the egg and says, "I can't believe it this egg is twenty-four carat gold!" The farmer is so excited. He exclaims loudly, "I'm saved, I'm saved." The farmer sells the golden egg to the jeweler, buys some food, and pays off the mortgage for that month on the farm. The farmer goes back to the goose and says, "Thank you so much. You have saved me. I truly appreciate you."

Another month passes and a farmer runs out of money again. However, this time he has become very smart. He goes back to the goose and says, "Goose, goose, can you lay another golden egg?" The goose makes a lot of noise, jumps off the nest, and there is another golden egg. The farmer gets a smart now and goes to the goose every single day to see if the goose will lay a golden egg. Every day, just like clockwork, the goose lays another golden egg. The farmer is thrilled. He pays off the entire mortgage on the farm. He builds a new barn. He buys some new farm equipment. He builds himself a new house. He is getting rich and he truly appreciates that goose.

More time passes. Now the farmer has more money than he knows what to do with. He starts to think, "I'm getting pretty rich. What should I do with all of my extra money? I know, I'll expand and buy some more land." A large plot of land right adjacent to his farm comes up for sale. The farmer goes down to find out how much the land costs. Unfortunately, he does not have enough money to buy the land so he goes back to the goose and says, "Goose, goose, can you lay two golden eggs a day?" The goose makes a lot of noise and jumps off the nest. The farmer eagerly reaches down into the nest but he finds only one golden egg. He is very frustrated because he really had his heart set on buying that piece of land. He thinks to himself, that land is perfect for me. It is right next to my farm. I have always wanted that piece of land.

He thinks as hard as he can to try to figure out a plan to get the land because he realizes that the land will not be on the market very long. If he does not buy the land now, someone else will buy it and he may never get the chance to own it. He will have to buy land that is not connected to his land. He paces back and forth in the barnyard trying to figure out a plan. He thinks for days and finally he has an idea. He thinks to himself, "I bet all of those eggs are inside that goose." He rushes over to the goose and grabs it by the neck. He chops off the goose's neck, rips it open and what does he find? Goose guts. What a mistake, he has just killed the goose that laid the golden egg. I am sure many of you recognize Aesop's ancient fable.

So what is the moral of the story for our organizations? Is there anyone in our organizations that we can consider the goose that lays the golden egg? Would it be the CEO? No, it is the workers. Every day we go to the workers and we ask, "Will you make a product? Will you do a service?" They say, "Yes sir, yes ma'am," and they get to work. At the end of the day, we sell the service they did or the product they made for gold, money. When an individual starts a business that is successful, they appreciate their workers. They think to themselves, "All of these people work for me and I get rich. I love these people; they are just like family to me."

Time passes and sometimes the owner realizes that there are many people out there who would like to work for him or her. They think to themselves, "There are a lot of people willing to work for me and I control all of these jobs." Sometimes they start to change the way they feel about their employees and start to take them for granted. More time passes and they think themselves, "I have built this business with my own to hands over these last twenty years. I deserve to reward myself. I think I will build myself might dream vacation home in Florida. It will only cost me two million dollars. Now how will I get my employees to work harder so I can get the money? I know. I will start a quota system. Maybe I'll call it a corporate objective."

The owner introduces a quota at one hundred units a week. The quota is reasonable and everyone hits quota every single day with regular effort. If everyone hits quota with regular effort do they feel competent? Yes they do. We know that when people feel competent their self-esteem increases. And when self-esteem increases, productivity increases. Now all of the employees are doing one hundred and ten units a week. This goes on for about a year and the owner says to him or herself, "My quota must be too low. I'll go-ahead and raise it up to one hundred and ten units a week." Since everybody already is doing one hundred and ten units a week, the quota is still reasonable. In addition, since the quota is higher, people feel good because they can do the higher quota. The employees' sense of competence increases, self-esteem increases and productivity increases again. Now people are getting close to maximum productivity and productivity increases only by five units a week.

As more time passes, the owner thinks to herself, I put in a quota and productivity increased. I increase the quota and productivity went up again. Let me see if I can stretch these employees a little bit. I will set the quota at one hundred and twenty units a week. Now the quota is too high. Still, the employees want to prove that they are competent so they do whatever it takes to hit that quota. They work overtime, they work during their breaks, they come in on weekends, or they take work home. This goes on for one, two, three, four, five, or six months. Then the employees get burnout and start to miss quota.

When employees start to miss quota the owner talks to managers and says, "What's wrong with these lazy employees? They hit quota for six months. Now they are slacking off. We better fire a few employees and get some new people in here who will work hard and hit that quota." The managers fire a few people and hire some new people. The new people want to prove that they are competent so they work hard. They do some overtime, they work over their breaks, they come in on weekends, or they take work home. This goes on for one, two, three, four, five, or six months. Then what happens? The new employees get burnout and start to miss quota. The owner rushes in and says, "There's something wrong with these lazy employees. Fire a few of them and get some new people in." Now the organization has turnover.

The alarm clock goes off in the morning and the employee jumps out of bed thinking to them self, "I can't wait to go into work and miss quota today!" What really happens is that they hit the snooze button repeatedly, and have no desire to get up and go to work. Alternatively, they call in to work and say, "I'm not feeling very well; I won't be able to make it in to that job that makes me feel so incompetent." While they probably will not say the part about feeling incompetent, that is how the quota makes them feel.

The employee comes home frustrated after a long week of missing quota. When they feel bad about themselves, do you think they keep it to themselves or do they share with anyone? Certainly, they share their frustration with their loved ones. When they are extremely frustrated, they may get angry quickly and get into fights with their spouse or significant other. They may yell at the kids. When we yell at our kids, they will often go to school and yell at other kids, get into fights and get bad grades.

If we run an organization with too high of quotas, what are we doing to the goose that lays the golden egg? Not only are we killing the goose that lays a golden egg, we are also pouring negativity into the entire society. Is this a responsible way to run an organization? Clearly, it is not. What if we are understaffed? If we are understaffed, isn't it just a hidden quota? When we are understaffed, everyone has to work harder to make up for the staffing problem. Many owners will say, "We can't afford to be fully staffed." I tell them that they cannot afford not to be fully staffed because when they are understaffed they are killing the goose that lays the golden egg.[11]

After teaching management seminars extensively throughout the United States, I have come to believe that at least fifty percent of the organizations in the United States are either understaffed or have too high of quotas. We must eradicate this system problem in our organizations by making sure that our organizations are fully staffed and that our quotas are not too high.

We do realize that some quotas are competence building. In our example, a quota of up to one hundred and ten units per week was competence building. It made people feel good about them self, have high self-esteem, and increased their productivity. A quota is competence building if all employees can hit quota every single day with regular effort. If an organization is going to have a quota, it must be competence building.

---

[11] Covey (1989)

Many managers do not like this idea because they feel they will lose the productivity of their high performers. The answer to this is to have a competence-building quota and give bonuses for productivity that is higher than the quota. For example, quota plus ten percent gets bonus a one percent bonus on the check that week. Quota plus twenty percent gets a two percent bonus on the check that week and so on. A quota plus bonus system motivates the peak performer to achieve in a high level and it does not destroy the sense of competence of the regular worker.

13

DEALING WITH CONFLICT

Dealing with conflict is the make or break skill. Very few managers are trained in it, and most of the training is inadequate because dealing with conflict is a complex issue. The biggest problem is the fact that each of us sees the world from our own individual framework called our worldview.

Much of our worldview is clear to us, like how we see others, our boss, employees, the government, our family, and ourselves. Most of us also understand that our family of origin had a lot to do with where our worldview came from. Generally, we either embrace or rebel against the worldview of our parents and other early childhood authority figures based on the feedback we receive from them. When we live up to their expectations for us, we receive positive reinforcement, and many times we respond by embracing their worldview. We fit in their world, and it is comfortable, therefore we embrace it as our own. On the other hand, when the parenting style of unconditional love is not used, and we do not live up to our family's expectations for us, we often receive negative reinforcement, and this generally creates rebellion.

During my many years of interacting with seminar participants and students, I have come to believe that most people were not raised with complete unconditional love. The more conditional early childhood authority figures were with love, the more difficulty the child has in adulthood, especially during stressful times of conflict.

We all have strategies to deal with conflict, and these strategies have names, avoiding, accommodating, competing, compromising, and collaborating. There are tests we can take to understand our natural conflict strategy choices. Most of us follow a pattern that we have learned from a parent or other family member. In general, our strategy works reasonably well for us. The real problem arises when our natural conflict strategy does not work. What do we do now?

Most of us have heard the old saying, "Deal with the problem, not the person." This is correct, but it is easier said than done, especially when someone verbally attacks us. When we are attacked on a personal level, our natural tendency is to protect ourselves. We may keep calm for a short while, but continued personal attacks often cause us to respond in kind. If we respond to a personal verbal attack with a verbal attack on the aggressor, a spiral of revenge is initiated.

For example, Jane and John are discussing a team assignment at work. Jane feels that John's work has some mistakes. When Jane speaks with John about correcting the mistakes, John feels threatened. Let us say that John has a deep subconscious need to be perceived by others as being perfect. We call this "face" or the "social mask." John interprets Jane's innocent, work-related assertion that he has made some mistakes in his work as a direct threat to his self-concept.

Psychologist tell us that if we believe something to be true, then it is true for us, and we will respond as if it is true whether it is objectively true or not. John believes that Jane has attacked him. He has an emotional response, and he loses grip of his ability to rationally respond to Jane. As the emotional part of John's brain kicks in, he will resort to either fight or flight. He may angrily accept the perceived attack and he may not fight back overtly if his perceived attacker is someone more powerful than himself (i.e. his boss). On the other hand, he might verbally attack back if he thinks he can win the fight. He might even verbally attack the more powerful person like his boss if he ends up in emotional meltdown and loses self-control.

If this happens in the workplace, he can kiss promotion goodbye. Very few bosses will promote someone who cannot control himself or herself. Therefore, learning how to handle conflict is make or break. Here the old saying is true that an eye for an eye makes everyone blind. The answer to the spiral of attacks is the wisdom to respond to an attack with an opposite response. This disarms our opponent. In conflict situations, we have to understand what is happening to us and we need a strategy to keep us from losing emotional control.

The good thing is that there are physical (physiological) signs that our emotions are taking over, like increased perspiration, shallow breathing, and rapid heartbeat. Understanding these signals can help us learn to consciously control the process. When we are in a conflict situation and we notice these physiological changes occurring in our body, we can step back and avoid the irrational emotional responses that can be triggered by conflict. By consciously moving back from the emotions of conflict, we can stay in rational control and choose our response to perceived attacks. Here is the key to success in conflict situations.

When we respond to perceived attacks opposite of our natural emotional response, we deescalate the conflict.

In our previous example, John notices the physical signs of conflict, like increased perspiration, shallow breathing, and rapid heartbeat as an emotional response to Jane's perceived attack. John consciously chooses to move back from the emotions of conflict and respond to Jane's perceived attack opposite of his natural emotional response. He says something like, "Let's go over are the mistakes that you found so that I can correct them." Now Jane and John can continue a civil conversation and solve the work problem. It does not even matter what Jane's actual motives were. She may have been attacking John's credibility to undermine him in the workplace. John's response shortcuts the attack whether it was perceived or real.

When dealing with conflict that does not seem to be resolvable, it is generally because we are not looking at the big picture. Each side has a position and the positions do not seem to be reconcilable. Traditional conflict resolution theory involves compromise. The problem here is that compromise leaves both sides less that fully satisfied with the outcome. Because of this dissatisfaction, compromise is just the beginning of a new form of the same old conflict. In recent years, conflict resolution theory has come to embrace a new concept; one that Dr. Steven Covey calls the third better alternative. So, how do we go about achieving the third better alternative?

When we are sure that there is no solution to a conflict, it is because we are firmly committed to our position. What we need to do is look past our position to the overarching interest that both sides can agree on. Naturally, we experience a great deal of conflict in the workplace, but the classic example of a child custody hearing will help us understand this concept.

In a divorce where both parents want full custody, each party's position is that they want the children. In the old way of thinking, one party will win and the other party will lose. When we move from the position to the interest, we embarking on true conflict resolution, a third better alternative.

In this example, if the parties have a reasonable level of emotional maturity, they would probably agree that they want what is best for the children. This is the mutual interest, the beginning of creating lasting conflict resolution. In my experience, these tough conflict situations generally require a non-biased third party mediator to help resolve the conflict because the parties are generally too emotionally involved to achieve third better solution conflict resolution on their own. People and circumstances are unique and a skilled mediator can help the parties craft a unique solution that will last.[12]

---

[12] I highly recommend taking a full course on how to deal with conflict in the workplace to expand on this short introduction.

14

WHAT IS YOUR PURPOSE IN LIFE?

Once you have figured out what your gifts are by understanding your own temperament, we need to figure out exactly what our purpose is in life. The way we understand our purpose is to align our talents and interests with a need in society. In his book Good to Great, Jim Collins speaks of what he calls the "hedgehog concept."[13] He says if you can align three things, you will find the purpose of your organization. The first question you want to ask yourself is "What are we deeply passionate about?" Second question you want to ask is "What can we be the best in the world

---

[13] Collins (2001)

at?" The third question is "What drives our economic engine?"

Dr. Stephen Covey in his book The 8th Habit speaks about finding and expressing your own voice. He says you need to align four things to find your voice. The four questions you need to ask yourself are, "What is my talent? What am I passionate about? Where is there a need in society that I can fill with my talent that I am passionate about? What can I do in good conscience?"

I like Dr. Covey's system because it includes morality when it says, "What can I do in good conscience?" In all fairness, Jim Collins is speaking about organizations while Dr. Covey is speaking about people but the concepts are the same. The main difference is between finding a need to fill and finding out what your organization can be the best in the world at. The problem here is that there will only be one best at each thing in the world and this concept is exclusionary and innately competition driven. The truth is that there are great needs in the world that can be filled by people who maximize their potential. Organizations and individuals do not need to be the best in the world to contribute.

15

THE FIVE AGES OF CIVILIZATION

In his book The 8th Habit, Dr. Covey talks about the different ages of civilization. He explains how wealth has continued to increase as society moves from age to age. He talks about how civilization has moved from the hunter gather age to the agricultural age, from the agricultural age to the industrial age and from the industrial age to the knowledge worker age. Through each age of civilization, society adjusted to a new reality and ninety percent of workers were downsized while society gained fifty times the productivity of the last age.

You see, farmers are fifty times more productive than hunter-gatherers are, factory workers are fifty times more productive than farmers are, and knowledge workers are fifty times more productive than factory workers are. If we want to enjoy the vast wealth that the enhanced productivity of knowledge workers is creating, we cannot treat them as thing the way many managers did with industrial workers. Knowledge workers will not give us the full benefit of their knowledge unless they believe they are being treated respectfully. We must learn to treat all employees as the truly valuable asset that they are.

As we move into the knowledge worker age, I believe that the world will move from the concept of competition to the concept of cooperation because true cooperation maximizes wealth. To cooperate we need to think in terms of inclusion. Our duty is to help people maximize their potential. In fact, Dr. Covey has a definition of leadership in his book The 8th Habit that I believe is the best definition of leadership I have ever heard; "Leadership is communicating to people their worth and potential so clearly that they come to see it in themselves."[14] If we follow Dr. Covey's advice to, "find our own voice and inspire others to find their voice," we will finally enter the age of wisdom.

[14] Covey (2004)

BIBLIOGRAPHY

Alessandra, T. (1996). *New Edition Relationship Strategies* [Sound Recording]. Wheeling, IL: Nightingale Conant.

Buckingham, M., & Coffman, C. (1999). *First, Break All the Rules: What the World's Greatest Managers Do Differently.* New York, NY: Simon & Schuster.

Collins, J. (2001). *Good to Great.* New York, NY: Harper Collins.

Covey, S. (1989). *7 Habits of Highly Effective People.* New York, NY: Free Press.

Covey, S. (2004). *The 8th Habit.* New York, NY: Free Press.

Deming, W. E. (2000). *The New Economics for Industry, Government, Education* (2nd ed.). Cambridge, MA: The Mit Press.

Ellis , A., & Ellis, D. J. (2011). *Therapy Rational Emotive Behavior Therapy (Theories of Psychotherapy)* (3rd ed.). Washington, DC: American Psychological Association.

Kohlberg, L. (1981). *The Philosophy of Moral Development: Moral Stages and the Idea of Justice (Essays on Moral Development, Volume 1)* (1st ed.). New York, NY: Harper & Row.

Myers, I. B. (1998). *Introduction to Type (6th ed.).* Mountain View, CA: CPP, Inc.

Nedivi, E. (2000, May 31). *Massachusetts Institute of Technology.* Retrieved from MIT News: http://newsoffice.mit.edu/2000/nedivi-0531

Tracy, B. (1984). *The Psychology of Achievement* [Sound Recording]. Wheeling, IL : Nightingale Conant.